Naaman's Servant Girl

By Cristina Marques

SCANDINAVIA

INTRODUCTION

Jesus said, "Become like little children." The Children of the Bible series puts attention on the littlest of Jesus' flock. Each of these characters has an inspiring story to tell. God used their lives to teach the world about his love. As you read these stories aloud, remember God's presence inside every child's spirit. The simplest stories sometimes hold the greatest power. May these stories be the beginning of a lifelong love of the Bible for your children. There is treasure to gain for young and old alike.

NAAMAN'S SERVANT GIRL

(2 KINGS 5:1-14)

Naaman was the captain of the Syrian army. On one of the raids by the army, a little girl was taken from Israel. She was brought back to Naaman's home. There she became a servant to Naaman's wife. She felt at home in the family.

Naaman was a brave man and a wonderful fighter. But he was unhappy because he had a disease called leprosy. His wife's little servant girl felt terrible about it. She didn't like to see people hurting.

The little servant girl went to Naaman's wife and told her, "I know of a prophet. He lives in my homeland. He can heal Naaman from his leprosy!" Naaman's wife began to feel hopeful. She told her husband what the servant girl had said.

So Naaman went to the king to ask permission to visit Israel where the prophet lived. "There is a prophet there," he told the king. "Perhaps he can heal me!"
The king was happy for Naaman. He sent him away with many gifts. "Give them to your healer," he said. So Naaman left for Israel.

When Naaman arrived, the prophet Elisha sent a messenger out to him. The messenger told Naaman to wash in the Jordan River seven times. But Naaman didn't listen because he was angry.

"Where is Elisha?" Naaman growled. "I've come all this way. I thought Elisha would be here. I thought he'd heal me right away!" Naaman stormed off in a rage.

The servants took Naaman aside. They calmed him down. "Don't you want to be healed?" they asked him. Naaman nodded. He went down to the Jordan River. There he washed himself seven times. When he stepped out of the water, his leprosy was gone!

Back home the little servant girl was happy for Naaman. She took care of him the best that she could. Every day he grew stronger.

The little servant girl knew God had healed Naaman. She had shared her love of God by telling him about the prophet of God. And God had worked a miracle that wonderful day!

NAAMAN'S SERVANT GIRL - COMPASSION

The little servant girl was a foreigner in a strange land. She was taken by Naaman's army and made to be a servant. But she was not angry or spiteful. When she saw Naaman in pain, she wanted to help him. This is what compassion is all about. She did what she could do. She told Naaman and his wife about God's healing power and the prophet Elisha. Naaman went to the prophet Elisha and was healed. When we see people who are hurting, we can show them we care. We can be an instrument of God's love just like the little girl.

© Scandinavia Publishing House
Drejervej 15,3 DK - Copenhagen NV Denmark
Tel. (+45) 3531 0330
www.scanpublishing.dk
info@scanpublishing.dk
All rights reserved.

Text: Cristina Marques
Illustrations and graphic design:
Belli Studio, Gao Hanyu
Translation: Ruth Marschalek, Lissa Jensen

Printed in China
ISBN: 978 87 7247 150 1